Living the Promises of Baptism

101 ideas for parents

A Washed and Welcome resource

AUGSBURG FORTRESS

washed and
welcome

Also available:
Welcome, Child of God (ISBN 978-1-4514-0133-2); a board book for infants
and toddlers
Washed and Welcome: A Baptism Sourcebook (ISBN 978-1-4514-0130-1)
Certificate for Sponsors (ISBN 978-1-4514-0132-5)

LIVING THE PROMISES OF BAPTISM
101 Ideas for Parents

Editor: Suzanne Burke
Writers: Melissa Bergstrom, Amanda Grell, Heather Hammond, Mary Lindberg, Betsy
Williams, David Batchelder
Cover illustration: Claudia McGehee
Interior art: Barbara Knutson and Claudia McGehee
Cover and interior design: Ivy Palmer Skrade

ISBN 978-1-4514-0131-8

'ed in the U.S.A.

14 13 12 11   3 4 5 6 7

Contents

Welcome

Being a parent is a profound spiritual journey that you share with your child. Parents are like John the Baptist, who "came as a witness to testify to the light, so that all might believe through him" without being the Messiah himself (John 1:7). Do not believe you must first have it all together to lead and nurture your child in faith. Accept your child's baptism as an invitation to grow in your own baptismal faith and calling.

This small book offers support, encouragement, and ideas for living the promises you made or will make at your child's baptism:

As you bring *your children* to receive the gift of baptism, you are entrusted with responsibilities:
  to live with *them* among God's faithful people,
  bring *them* to the word of God and the holy supper,
  teach *them* the Lord's Prayer, the Creed, and the Ten
      Commandments,
  place in *their* hands the holy scriptures,
  and nurture *them* in faith and prayer,
  so that *your children* may learn to trust God,
  proclaim Christ through word and deed,
  care for others and the world God made,
  and work for justice and peace.

Do you promise to help *your children* grow in the Christian faith and life?
I do.
(*Evangelical Lutheran Worship*, p. 228)

5

This book also invites you to remember the promises God makes to us in baptism:

> God, who is rich in mercy and love, gives us a new birth into a living hope through the sacrament of baptism. By water and the Word God delivers us from sin and death and raises us to new life in Jesus Christ. We are united with all the baptized in the one body of Christ, anointed with the gift of the Holy Spirit, and joined in God's mission for the life of the world. (*Evangelical Lutheran Worship*, p. 227)

Living the Promises of Baptism is arranged into ten major sections, with ideas identified by their appropriateness for various age groups, infants through age 12:

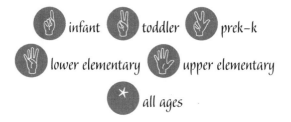

How do we get children on board with family rituals like those described in this book? While it is easier to enlist younger children in family rituals, it is never too late to begin. Begin with ideas that fit into activities that are already natural to your family, like bedtimes, family meals, or holiday celebrations. Try only one or two ideas at first. Choose activities that relate to your child's particular interests or concerns. If you have children of widely different ages, choose an activity that the oldest child can enjoy without feeling immature. Don't feel

6

defeated if you try something that doesn't receive a positive response. An idea may require adaptation or flexibility before it works for you, or it may not work at all for you. Try something else. The same idea may work perfectly well when your child is a different age or family circumstances change. Be patient and persistent, and trust the Holy Spirit to lead and inspire. It takes a short time for children to remember a family ritual as "the way we've always done it."

God calls us to be faithful spiritual teachers to our kids, day by day, year by year. God strengthens us to do our work—reading Bible stories to our kids, praying with them, caring for God's creation with them, and teaching them right and wrong. And one day, as they grow, our kids will be ready to say, "God loves us," with their words, their choices, their hopes, and their outreach. And on that day, the God-and-parents team will smile. Blessings on the way.

Mealtime

all ages

1. Here are some simple prayers that you and your children can pray together at mealtime. Hold hands around the table as you pray, or teach your children to do "praying hands"—hands folded together.

Come, Lord Jesus, be our guest,
and let these gifts to us be blessed.

Blessed be God who is our bread;
may all the world be clothed and fed.

May there be a goodly share
on every table everywhere.

Once your children are comfortable with the first verse, add a second, then a third. All three verses can be sung to the tune of "Twinkle, Twinkle, Little Star."

Another simple, spoken grace before each meal is "Give us today our daily bread." Applying this most tangible part of the Lord's Prayer will help children realize its meaning, recognize it when they hear it in church, and pray the words themselves.

Meal prayer might be introduced with these words used each week in church: One member says, "The Lord be with you"; the rest reply, "And also with you." The first speaker then says, "Let us give thanks to the Lord our God." The rest answer, "It is right to give our thanks and praise." By using this "church" language at mealtime, we remember that what we do in one place is closely related to what we do in another. In addition, it helps our children learn this language by heart even before they are able to read it in a church bulletin. Finally, this ritual and these words imply that the family dinner table is very much like the table around which God's family gathers with the risen Christ to share bread and wine.

 infant

2. Using sign language with an infant can be a beautiful way for parent and child to communicate. At the beginning and end of each meal, use two simple movements to remind you and your child how God blesses us with food: "Thank you" (almost like blowing a kiss,

9

bring your hand—palm in—from your mouth out in one gesture) and "God" (bring your hand—palm to the side—down from above your forehead to your mouth). Gently help your infant make these movements and demonstrate them many times—pretty soon he will join in the dance of grace.

 infant

3. Cook the carrots for hours (!) until they are soft. Blend them to shiny smoothness. Scoop up a colorful little plop of pureed carrots and put it in your baby's mouth. Watch the surprise in her eyes as she tastes her first solid food! Wow, this tastes new and yummy and . . . oops! The whole spoonful of orange carrots comes back out of your baby's mouth! God spoon-feeds us the grace of love and forgiveness, a delicious treat. We know it tastes sweet, but somehow the goodness throws us at first. We spit it out. God tries again and again, until we are fed.

 toddler prek-k

4. Keep photos of family and friends in a basket near the dining table. Holiday cards and birth or adoption announcements work especially well for this activity. At suppertime, ask your child to pull out one photo, talk about who it is, and say a short prayer for that person or family. This practice keeps kids connected with faraway relatives and provides a jumping-off point for family prayer times.

prek-k

5. Washing hands before every meal makes good health sense. Make it more fun by turning it into a playful reminder of God's grace and forgiveness in the water of baptism. Sing "I am washing in the love of God" to the tune of "We Are Marching in the Light" (*Evangelical Lutheran Worship* #866) for a little good, clean fun!

 prek-k lower

6. Special meals at home prepare young children to understand the special meal of holy communion. Engage your child in preparations for special family meals by asking him to decorate and set the table, choose special foods, make placemats, light candles (with help), and choose a table grace and teach it to guests. Consider using hymns or songs to connect God's table to the family table, such as the first stanza of "As the Grains of Wheat" or "Now the Feast and Celebration" (*Evangelical Lutheran Worship* #465, 167). With help, your child could create a table card with the words for each guest.

 prek-k lower  upper

7. Martin Luther engaged students and family gathered for meals with lively conversations that became known as "Table Talk." Plan your own Table Talk tradition by introducing a common question or topic for conversation at mealtime. You may begin as simply as asking each person to tell about one "high point" in the day and one "low point"

in the day. After attending worship, ask each person to talk about one thing she learned, heard, or appreciated, or one thing she remembers from scriptures, prayer, or sermon. During Lent, with older children, read a question from the Small Catechism (*Evangelical Lutheran Worship*, pp. 1160–67). Ask family members, "What does this mean to you?"

The Talking Spoon is a playful way to manage distraction, improve conversation, and encourage everyone's participation as you introduce Table Talk. Decorate a large wooden spoon or spatula. Pass it from one person to the next. The person holding the Talking Spoon may talk, as long as she remains on the subject. When finished, she can pass it to another person, who continues the conversation.

Bedtime

 toddler prek–k  lower upper

8. Bedtime prayer works deep in a child's consciousness and has the power to build a habit of trust that can last a lifetime. Here are several bedtime prayers that easily can be memorized through repetition and prayed by parent and child together.

Be our light in the darkness, O Lord,
and in your great mercy
defend us from all perils and dangers of this night;
for the love of your only Son,
our Savior Jesus Christ.

We bless you, God, for the day just spent,
for laughter, tears, and all you've sent.
Grant us, Good Shepherd, through this night,
a peaceful sleep till morning light.

Send angels, Lord, around us here,
to keep our dreaming free from fear.
When morning comes, to bring the day,
show us how to follow your way.

Dear Jesus,
as a hen covers her chicks with her wings to keep them safe,
protect us this night under your golden wings,
for your mercy's sake.

9. As the last step in your child's bedtime routine, stroke your thumb across his forehead, repeatedly forming a cross. This soothing touch calms your child while mimicking the cross traced on his head by the pastor at his baptism. Speak a simple remembrance of God's love and the love of those around him, such as "You are a child of God," "Remember your baptism and be thankful. You belong to God," or "Remember that you are baptized and Jesus loves you. Mama loves you; Daddy loves you; *brothers'/sisters' names* love you; Grandma loves you," and so on. If your child is old enough, let him add names to the list. Listen as the list grows and changes from day to day.

These words recall for us all the power and significance of our Christian identity. With this identity comes God's faithful promise and presence from which nothing can separate us—not darkness, not sleep, not fear, not even death itself.

10. Read or sing the board book *Welcome, Child of God* as a bedtime lullaby (Augsburg Fortress, 2011). The brief text may be sung to the tune AR HYD Y NOS, sometimes known as "All through the Night" or "Go, My Children, with My Blessing." Let the words become a prayer for your child: "When the world feels wide around you / When the dark of night surrounds you / We are here to tend and guide you."

11. Finish your story and song time together by singing "Jesus Loves Me," inserting the name of your precious child in each line: "Jesus loves *name*, this I know. . . . Yes, Jesus loves *name*!"

15

 infant

12. Sleep, delicious sleep . . . where has it gone? Suddenly you are getting up at all hours to feed and comfort a baby. As you stumble around with your eyes half closed in the middle of the night, you are living out the call to nurture your child. The power of love makes you willing to make the sacrifice. And good news—God is up! God is always available.

Around the table, around the room, around the circle you walk and walk, patting your baby's back. Your repetitive motion works very well with the rhythms of simple hymns or Bible songs. Sing "Jesus Loves Me," "Amazing Grace," and "This Little Light of Mine" to your child (and to yourself).

Whisper prayers for your baby. Hearing your own words will teach you what you believe about God and how you want your baby to know God. As you pace each lap, pray for a different person in your baby's life. It's actually good that you're half asleep, because prayers are about leaning and trusting, not just about the efficiency of our awake times of day.

 toddler   prek–k

13. One of the easiest ways to pray with your toddler is to pray happiest-and-saddest prayers together. Each person recalls a happy and sad moment from his day. St. Ignatius actually recommended this way of praying. He called this the Examen prayer, because it's a way to examine God's actions in our lives. At the end of the prayer, you say, "God is with us through happy and sad times. Amen."

Even very young children embrace the practice of happiest-and-saddest prayers. By noting both our highs and lows, we are honoring each day of our lives, rather than just letting them whoosh by. After praying the Examen prayer night after night, you begin to recognize patterns in your life and your child's life of what brings you joy and what challenges or disappoints you. Praying the Examen prayer opens little windows in the soul of your family to share God's ways.

 lower  upper

14. The day your child was baptized, the pastor spoke words from Isaiah 11:2 as a blessing: "Sustain *name* with the gift of your Holy Spirit: the spirit of wisdom and understanding, the spirit of counsel and might, the spirit of knowledge and the fear of the Lord, the spirit of joy in your presence" (*Evangelical Lutheran Worship*, p. 231). Those same words will be repeated on your child's affirmation of baptism (confirmation) day. Help her grow into that blessing by using these words as part of a bedtime ritual. You might lay one or both hands on her head as you speak this blessing.

Caring for the Body

infant   toddler

15. At bath time, try singing this catchy rhyme to the tune of "Jesus Loves Me."

Jesus washed your sins away
on your blessed baptismal day.
In the bath I wash you too
and remind you God loves you.
Yes, you are baptized,
yes, you are baptized,
yes, you are baptized, and God's love is with you.

Or try this song to the tune of "Ring around the Rosie."

Bring us to God's waters,
all you sons and daughters.
Splashes, splashes,
God's love comes down.

infant

16. Is there anything as slippery as a newborn baby? Baby's first baths are magical and nerve-wracking. It's so amazing to see your new little person lying on a fluffy towel and wiggling his little body. But trying to figure out how to hold your baby for a bath can be awkward. Sometimes it works best to just get in the tub with your baby so you can support him with your body. As you hold this little being who can't even sit yet, imagine God's arms around you. God holds and supports us! God bathed us in the waters of baptism and brought us through to new life.

19

toddler prek-k

17. Bath time, when parent and child are both relaxed and having fun together, can be a delightful opportunity to connect the pleasurable experience of bathing with God's warm, supporting love poured out in baptism. Pouring clear warm water on your child's head, say, "This is just like Pastor did when you were baptized, so you'll always know God loves you!"

 infant

18. Cherish your child's beautiful body by singing during a diaper change or clothes change, or provide a calming massage for your baby. We are all part of Christ's body. Sing about each part to the tune "The Wheels on the Bus."

Your soft, tickly toes are the body of Christ,
body of Christ, body of Christ.
Your soft, tickly toes are the body of Christ,
all of your life.

Your cute, chubby nose . . .
Your big, strong arms . . .
Your stinky, smelly feet . . .
Your long, wiggly fingers . . .

infant

19. Whenever you find a mirror—in the bathroom, in the bedroom, in the hallway—show your child the reflection of this "child of God." Remind her of her name and identity: "*Name*, child of God, you are loved!" Having a mirror by the changing table or even hung on the wall (securely!) right at your infant's eye level can be a blessed distraction during diaper changes, dressing, or nail trimming. Adding a small cross, rainbow, or shell-shaped stickers to the mirror can add visual reminders of God's promises in baptism.

 infant

20. Baby socks are so cute that we don't even mind doing the laundry! Place one of your socks next to your baby's sock. "Your word is a lamp to my feet and a light to my path" (Psalm 119:105). Thank God for all the places your feet have carried you, and imagine all the places your baby's feet might carry her. Ask each day where God wants you and your baby to walk. The next time you pick up a stray sock off the floor, remember God's word: "How beautiful upon the mountains are the feet of the messenger who announces peace" (Isaiah 52:7).

infant

21. Do you "wear" the good news of your baptism every day? One of the simplest, but most important, ways to teach our children about baptism is to smile! Smile at that squirming baby as you try to wrangle on his clothes. Use your face to show your child what you believe—that God's grace enfolds us. God invites us to pass on the gift of faith to our children. We are loved, forgiven, and saved by God. So relax! God has done the big work of saving us—now if God could just keep this baby still!

 infant

22. It's a scary moment. What will you find? What have you forgotten is in there? It's the moment when you decide to clean out the diaper bag! There's nothing like a diaper bag to teach us about sin and grace. No matter how cute and clean the outside of that diaper bag looks when you first get it as a baby shower gift, sooner or later those real-life baby stains begin to leak through. That juice stuck on the bottom of the bag reminds us that life is sticky and messy. Those dirty, smelly diapers remind us that we can all smell less than sweet.

Teaching your child about faith happens as you swab out that diaper bag. Your child sees that we have to clean up our messes, again and again. But we don't have to let all those messes get us down. Our dirt and sin are not the end of the story. Through baptism, God set us free from being measured by our illusions of perfection. God knows exactly how we look and smell—and loves us even more than we love our messy little babies. Pass the wipes—this good news is bringing me to tears!

Play

prek-k   lower   upper

23. The next time a soft, warm rain shower (with no thunder or lightning!) is falling, send your child out to play in it, and for extra fun, join him! Urge him to see how many raindrops he can catch on his tongue. Look for rainbows. Help the worms to higher ground. Then tell your child about how the warm, fresh water reminds you of God's love splashing all around at a baptism. All who attend a baptism get soaked in God's love, even if they never touched the water!

Some elementary-aged children love a thrillingly LOUD rainstorm, others not so much. Whatever the preferences of your child, a powerful, cleansing rainstorm can be a moment to remember the strong, cleansing love of God promised to you and your child in baptism. A vigorous rain settles the dust and cleans every leaf and blade of grass. So, too, God's baptismal washing "settles the dust" of everyday distractions and disappointments by reminding us whose we are. You and your child belong all to God, all the time, and that's really all that matters. Like a strong rain, God's love in baptism cleans away the mean and selfish things we do so that we can start fresh.

infant

24. Reminding your child of God's love is easy—every time you say, "Peek-a-boo," just add the rhyme, "God loves you!"

infant

25. There's a special kind of God time called kairos time. Kairos time doesn't run by the clock; it runs by God's ways of life slowly unfolding. There's a special kind of infant time called baby swing time. Baby swing time definitely doesn't run by the clock; it runs by baby saying,

"More, more!" God and your baby are inviting you to slow down and remember what's really important. So keep pushing that swing and stop worrying, at least for a moment, about where else you should be. Breathe deep. Find the wellspring of patience and grace you received in baptism. Give thanks that God always has time for us.

 infant

26. One of the first reflexes a baby practices is to hold on to your finger. Your little one is already learning to trust that you will be there for them to hold on to. When we baptize our baby, we promise to proclaim Christ in word and deed. That simply means that when your baby holds on to your finger you can connect their action with your words about trust: "Moooooommeee loves you. Daaaaaaaaddeee loves you. God loves you." See if you can get your baby giggling by repeating this happy news. Or sing "This Little Light of Mine" with your index finger extended upwards as a "candle" for baby to grasp and hold.

 toddler

27. Make it simple! Toddle around the block with your toddler. Leave your watch at home and simply go at her pace. This idea is certainly simple, but that doesn't mean it's easy! When you focus on your child instead of your phone, your friend, or your coffee, you must discover her little way of seeing the world and her style of communication. Even if you don't know it, you are teaching your toddler about prayer. When you give her your full attention, you're demonstrating what God always gives each of us.

toddler

28. If there's one place where toddlers learn the most about justice, it's the playground. Where else do you have to learn to share, make friends, work it out, and treat each other with fairness? Encourage your toddler to take turns at the playground and share the swings and slides. Stay calm, and he will too. Bring a friend to play with and snacks and water for tired kids. Observe how your child interacts with others, and help him make good choices. The playground may be the place for child's play, but the skills kids learn there are skills we all need for our entire lives.

 toddler prek–k

29. When you and your child are outside blowing bubbles, try saying some bubble prayers. Use a bubble wand to blow bubbles up to the sky. Imagine that they are floating up to God. With each puff of bubbles, say a prayer that will float up with them. This is a great chance to model the language your child may have heard in worship during the prayers. After the bubbles have all floated away, say, "Hear our prayer." Then blow another set of bubbles to the sky, repeating, "Hear our prayer," each time. The giggles and excitement of the bubble blowing will model for your child the joy and fun of praying and praising God.

 prek–k

30. Many children love the feeling of floating in water. Learning that water will support them helps children feel more comfortable in water and prepares them for learning to swim. The next time you are playing in a pool or a lake with your child, invite her to experience it: "Feel how the water holds you up? The water carries you; it even carries me!" Connect the experience to baptism: "This pool reminds me of God's love; it carries us too. When you were baptized you were too little to swim in a pool, but not anymore!"

 prek–k

31. Playing with clay makes fun time out of rainy days or anytime your child needs to be indoors for quiet play. As you work the clay, ask, "If you could make a world, what kind of creatures would you make? The more outrageously fun, the better! When the time seems right, mention, "When God chose what kind of creatures to make, God chose to make you. Pretty special."

27

lower *upper*

32. The next time your family visits a museum, be on the lookout for baptismal artifacts or depictions of baptisms from long ago. Among the artifacts on display at small local museums, you may find the baptismal font from a pioneer church or a well-worn record book listing the names of baptized babies. Large metropolitan museums may display carved fonts, exquisite ewers (the pitcher used for baptismal water), or even silver "shells" sometimes used in baptisms. Point out the artifacts to your child, and together guess how old the babies (whose baptisms used the displayed objects) would be now: 117? 312? 1,427? Wow, that's *old!* Remark how all the people baptized with the articles you see are like relatives you've never met, people who trust God, just like you and your child do.

upper

33. Soccer, football, hockey, baseball: these great sports attract millions of children. By the upper elementary ages, some kids have become quite competitive, and others take it to heart when they don't perform as well as they hoped. Teammates and other parents can sometimes be harsh when a mistake costs the team. This is a good time to begin learning how to forgive one's self, and move on. God's grace in baptism shows us how. Talk to your child. There is nothing you can do, not even missing the perfect scoring opportunity, that can shake God's love. Maybe a teammate or a coach is disappointed for a time, but so what? God is proud: you showed effort, courage, and persistence. You got out there and tried; that makes God (and me) proud of you.

Faith at Home

29

infant

34. At the time of your baby's birth or baptism, ask significant people in your baby's life to write a prayer for him on a large note card or colorful piece of card stock. You can send these cards out by mail or pass them out at the baptism. When you have collected the prayers, and have been moved and amazed by them, place the prayer cards in a special memory book, perhaps with pictures of the people who wrote the prayers. Later you can page through this book with your infant, exclaiming, "There's Grandma. She loves you." "There's your godfather. He prays for you." Or you can frame the prayers and pictures and hang them in your child's room. Your baby will sleep and play surrounded by prayers.

At his baptism, your child may have received a banner, garment, or towel with his name and baptism date on it. Display this in your child's room as a constant reminder of his baptism.

 infant

35. Please and thank you—we teach our little ones to say these important words very early in their lives. Stroller prayers teach us parents to say please and thank you to God. When we push our precious sleeping bundle, all tucked into the stroller, we sigh a deep, grateful prayer. *Thank you, thank you, thank you, God, for this unimaginable gift.* And half an hour later, when our newborn wakes up half a mile from home and screeches to be fed or changed, we repeat a fervent prayer. *Please, please, please, God, help me push this stroller as fast as I can!*

 toddler prek-k

36. Make sure your child has access to a story Bible such as the *Spark Story Bible* (Augsburg Fortress, 2009). Read and talk about the stories often, every day if possible. On car trips, put the Bible next to your child's car seat so that she can reach it and flip through it on the drive. Read a story or two from the Bible each night before bed.

 toddler prek-k

37. Your child may be learning prayers at school or Sunday school. Ask him about the prayers, and use those prayers in your home. Or encourage your child to create an original prayer with your help. There are four basic types of prayer that all children should learn:

Adoration: You're awesome, God!

Confession: I'm sorry.

Thanksgiving: Thank you.

Supplication: Please.

Begin teaching your child these types of prayers using the following examples:

Adoration: Dear God, I love you. You are an awesome God! Amen.

Confession: Dear God, I'm sorry for _____. Please forgive me. Amen.

Thanksgiving: Thank you, God, for _____. Amen. (Let your child fill in the blank with things he is thankful for.)

Supplication: Dear God, please help people who are sick. Amen.

Let your child add any requests that he has for himself or others.

🤟 toddler ✌️ prek-k

38. Keep a plastic dishpan and towel handy near the door of your house. On warm days when your child comes inside after playing barefoot, give her a foot wash to remove sand, dirt, and grass from her feet and legs. Take your time, gently stroking her calves, heels, and toes, rinsing them with soothing water. This activity recalls the tradition that many churches practice of washing one another's feet on Maundy Thursday—the Thursday before Easter. If this is a ritual your child has experienced at church, remind her of that experience. Quote Jesus' words to his disciples: "So if I, your Lord and Teacher, have washed your feet, you also ought to wash one another's feet" (John 13:14). Later on, when you are indoors, read her the complete story of Jesus washing the disciples' feet (John 13:1-17). Don't be surprised if she wants to wash your feet in return!

✌️ prek-k 🖐️ lower 🖐️ upper

39. As you introduce your child to the Ten Commandments, read Martin Luther's Small Catechism to remind yourself of how Luther explains the commandments (*Evangelical Lutheran Worship*, pp. 1160–61). Notice how Luther puts a positive spin on each commandment so that the result is uplifting and life-giving rather than a list of no-nos. Read the story of Moses and the Ten Commandments to your child from his picture Bible so he can hear the whole list and the context it came from.

As older children begin to question household rules, use the Ten Commandments and Luther's explanations to create a family covenant. Point out the question "What does this mean?" after each commandment. The answer describes what God desires in our relationships with God and one another. Ask, "What do you think this means for our family?" Your child may answer, "I don't know," rather than risk giving a wrong answer, or give you the answer he believes you expect. If your child believes it is your question too, he'll be more likely to engage the question helpfully. Begin with a baptismal affirmation of your life together as a family, such as "Each of us is a child of God through baptism, and this is how we will live together." Ask your child to create an attractive copy of the covenant for everyone to sign. Place it where everyone can see it, and refer to it to affirm ways family members keep the covenant.

prek–k lower upper

40. During the evening, at mealtime, or before bedtime routines begin, share highs and lows from the day with your family. Each person present, parents included, shares a high point and a low point of her day. Depending on the person and the day, answers may be funny, heartfelt, or mundane. This activity can also be done one-on-one by a parent and child during bath time. If sharing your highs and lows seems awkward at first, stick with it. It will soon become a highly anticipated part of your family's day. When you have guests, invite them to share something too. This communication-building activity can start as soon as children are verbal enough to understand the concept and can continue through high school and beyond.

prek–k  lower upper

41. One of the great gifts we can give our children is the ability to recall God's scriptural promises during personal crises and at times of joy, loss, doubt, or loneliness. Consider, for example, the reassurance offered in these words from Psalm 23: "Even though I walk through the darkest valley, I fear no evil; for you are with me." With regular guidance and encouragement from their parents, children can commit such wonderful words and promises to memory. Here are suggestions for a few significant scripture passages that children and adults might learn:

Genesis 12:2-3	Luke 4:18-19	Romans 12:1-2
Psalm 23	John 3:16	Ephesians 2:8-10
Psalm 121	John 11:25-26	Philippians 1:6
Proverbs 3:5-6	John 13:34-35	Philippians 4:6-7
Isaiah 40:30-31	John 15:9-10	Colossians 3:1-3
Isaiah 41:10	John 17:20-21	Hebrews 11:1-2
Matthew 6:33	Acts 10:43	Hebrews 12:1-3
Matthew 11:28-29	Romans 8:37-38	

Families might learn these passages by reciting them together—one passage each day for a week—as part of their mealtime prayer.

prek-k  lower

42. Share an energizing morning stretch with your child to start the day. Use this prayer attributed to Saint Patrick.

Christ be with me,
(cross hands to each shoulder and hug yourself)

Christ within me,
(still hugging shoulders, twist to the right and then to the left)

Christ behind me,
(stretch arms behind, grasping hands behind back)

Christ before me,
(reach arms straight in front)

Christ beside me,
(stretch arms like an airplane, tilt to the right, and then left)

Christ beneath me,
(crouch and touch floor with fingertips)

Christ above me,
(reach for the sky)

Christ in hearts of all that love me.
(end with a warm hug)

35

lower upper

43. Children learn parts of the liturgy easily during weekly worship. Notice pieces that your child enjoys most and suggest them at other times during the week. You don't have to sing especially well to sing them together! For example, the refrain "Glory to God" from any musical setting can become a spontaneous "Wow!" to good news.

lower upper

44. A child with chronic illness or disability may spend a lot of time focused on what's wrong with him. Baptism offers a different vision and hope for a child and family living with disability, and for the Christian community formed by baptism. God claims us and bestows the gifts of the Spirit without regard to abilities or disabilities. Jesus welcomes those who are weakest and makes them a living sign of the kingdom of God in our midst (Mark 9). Read the order for Holy Baptism in *Evangelical Lutheran Worship* (pp. 227–31) to find a blessing to remind yourself and your child of this hope. "Let your light so shine before others that they may see your good works and glorify your Father in heaven" or "Child of God, you have been sealed by the Holy Spirit and marked with the cross of Christ forever" work well as a bedtime blessing or an off-to-school blessing, spoken while tracing the sign of the cross on your child's forehead. Worship with your child and ask your pastor to help arrange whatever adaptations your family may need to participate comfortably. In baptism, your child belongs.

36

 lower  upper

45. Children can learn about Jesus as the bread of life by making bread at home. Choose a simple whole wheat bread recipe and ask your child to help measure and add ingredients. Read each of these verses as the ingredient is added.

Yeast: Matthew 13:33
Salt: Mark 9:50
Flour: Psalm 81:16
Honey: Psalm 119:103
Water: Revelation 21:6
Oil: James 5:14 (This may require an explanation that oil was used as a sign of healing.)
When the bread is finished: John 6:35

As you share the fresh baked bread, talk about God's goodness in providing us every good gift we need to live out our baptism. "God is so good, God gives us . . . "

upper

46. It happens in every family, to all of us. We did something we knew we shouldn't have. Then everyone has to find a way forward together. As a parent, you know your child must take responsibility for unacceptable actions; you know that misbehaving has consequences. Forgiveness doesn't make the act suddenly okay, but it does create a way forward. Lead the way by forgiving your child. You might say, "This whole thing leaves me feeling (*name your feeling*). I don't like that. But I do forgive you, right here and now. You know why? Because I've made mistakes too. God has always forgiven me, so I'm forgiving you. God loves us even when we screw up. There will still be consequences for what you have done, but we can and will get past this." Be careful not to make your forgiveness contingent on your child's apology. Your child won't *feel* forgiven until she feels sorry enough to apologize, but your forgiveness, like God's forgiveness, cannot be bought with an apology. Forgiveness is a gift, won by Jesus, poured out on you and your child in baptism.

 upper

47. Nurturing a child in faith is not always a matter of *doing* the right activities. The older child's world is increasingly scheduled and task oriented. Turn off electronics and screens for a while. Cultivate time spent driving, waiting at the doctor's office, or in line at the grocery store as an invitation to conversation. Allow time for questions to grow. Ask your child for his thoughts and opinions. Refrain from critiquing answers. Express appreciation.

38

Celebrating Seasons

all ages

48. Make a special place for your infant or toddler to celebrate Advent and prepare for Christmas without the danger and fragility of the traditional tree and ornaments. Decorate a corner or central spot of your home with nontoxic garland, and place a baby cradle or toy crèche there (or make a simple one with blankets and a cardboard box). Help your child place symbols of the season inside the crèche (and take them out and put them back again!): kid-friendly nativity sets, baby dolls, toy animals, and boxes with lids for "gifts" from the wise men.

For older children, provide a crèche at their eye level that is okay for them to touch and play with. Put up only the stable or backdrop to the manger scene. Each day, read a verse or two of the Christmas story (Luke 2:1-20) and bring in the appropriate characters from the story. Mary and Joseph arrive (with a donkey if your crèche has one) before Christmas. Baby Jesus arrives on Christmas, then angel, shepherds, magi. Let your children move the figures around and play-act with them. Read the Christmas story over and over to help your children learn it well.

When the crèche is first arranged in its place, a prayer might be spoken or prayed in unison, such as the following.

Faithful God, who blesses us in our waiting,
bless, too, this crèche, which awaits your Son.
As the holy family journeys to this manger,
prepare our hearts to welcome his presence.
Through Jesus Christ our Lord.

toddler   prek–k   lower   upper

49. The discipline of Advent waiting can be captured in Christmas decorating when decorating is carried out in steps. Rather than putting up everything in a mad frenzy when you finally find time to do it, designate specific days for progressive stages of decoration so your home reflects the coming of Christmas rather than just its arrival. For example, you might set aside a day for starting a Christmas card display (that can be added to as more cards come in); another day can be designated for trimming the mantel; and one day could be spent putting up and decorating the tree. Families also might choose to decorate the house in stages—first the front door and entranceway, next the hallway, then the family room, and so on—climaxing with the trimming of the tree. By extending this preparation time, you will discover a sense of growing anticipation as well as a meaningful progression through Advent into Christmas.

 toddler prek–k lower  upper

50. During Advent, the Advent wreath can form a focal point for family worship, especially if the wreath is set in the center of the dinner table. The lighting of the wreath at each evening meal can lead into a prayer or meditation that reflects the meaning of Advent. When the wreath is first lit each year, a blessing such as this might be said.

Faithful God, who sent us Jesus,
make this wreath smile with joy
and these candles burn brightly
with the truth of your word.
Through Jesus Christ our Lord.

41

toddler prek–k lower upper

51. There is a rich tradition of house blessing at Epiphany, for the festival coincides with the arrival of a new year. This blessing can beautifully supplement the "20 + C + M + B + (*current year*)" markers over the doorposts. Cut a small evergreen branch from a bush or tree and use it to sprinkle "water of blessing," evoking our identity as those God has welcomed in baptism. Evergreens symbolize the power of eternal life because they never lose their green, even in the dead of winter. Here is an example of a house blessing ritual.

One person may lead, or leadership may be shared.
Peace be to this house and to all who enter here.
A reading from Proverbs: By wisdom a house is built and through understanding it is established; through knowledge its rooms are filled with rare and beautiful treasures" (Proverbs 24:3-4).
Let us pray: Gracious God, as a shining star once guided the wisemen to the birthplace of the infant Jesus, so enable those who dwell here to be your light in the world; through Jesus Christ we pray.
Amen.

Mark the door with 20 + C + M + B + (last two digits of the current year). Join hands and pray.
Sovereign God, we pray that you will bless this home and all who live here with your gracious presence. May your love be our inspiration, your wisdom our guide, your truth our light, and your peace our benediction; through Jesus Christ we pray.
Amen.

Pray the Lord's Prayer.

Make the sign of the cross on your children's foreheads in remembrance of their baptism. Invite them to do the same for you and for each other.
May the Lord watch over our going out and our coming in, from this time forth and forevermore.
Amen.

Singing a hymn such as "We Three Kings," journey with your family through the house, sprinkling water in each room. Each child may sprinkle his or her own room. Include the pets too—no one is left out!

 toddler prek–k  lower upper

52. Celebrated on January 6, Epiphany invites families to participate in rich, imaginative, and playful rituals. With a little planning, you can incorporate a number of delightful traditions into your family celebrations. In some European homes, it is customary at Epiphany to mark the lintel above doorways with symbols of blessing. Invite your children to mark your own front door with these symbols: the date, the initials of traditional names for the three magi (Caspar, Melchior, and Balthasar), and four crosses. Order these symbols in the following way, 20 + C + M + B + (*last two digits of the current year*), with the four crosses representing the four seasons. In the new year, this marking serves as a blessing over the entire household. Be artistic and creative. The marking may be made with chalk or on a piece of cardboard that has been decorated with colored markers and designs.

 toddler prek–k

53. Ash Wednesday worship can leave young children with lots of questions. *What is that dirt on your forehead?* Tell your little one that the "dirt" is a reminder sign about Jesus and love. After Ash Wednesday worship, play a new chapter of church at home. Put some water or olive oil into a small bowl. Preschoolers can mark the foreheads of their stuffed animals, action figures, and dolls, saying, "Remember God loves you."

prek–k  lower

54. Christians practice three faith disciplines during Lent (the six weeks before Easter): prayer, fasting, and sharing. Preschoolers can practice all three of these Lenten disciplines at home.

Prayer: Preschoolers love to name colors, and Lent has a color. Lent is purple, like a king's robe. Jesus is our King. Cut strips of purple paper to make a day-by-day paper prayer chain. Each night during Lent, name a special prayer with your child and write it on a purple strip. Loop each prayer into the growing purple prayer chain.

As a variation on this idea for older children, your links could include Lenten practices rather than prayers. Some links will give your child something to do that day as she prepares for Jesus' death on Good Friday and resurrection at Easter. Here are some examples:

- Ask your pastor why we put ashes on our foreheads during Ash Wednesday worship.
- Choose and drop off three items today for your local food pantry.
- Check out a book about Easter from your library to learn how Easter is celebrated in other countries.
- Read John 13:1-17 in your Bible and wash one another's feet.
- Wear Lent's color (purple) today.

Fasting: Prepare a simple "cross" dinner during Lent with your preschooler. Make sandwiches and cut them into cross shapes. Crisscross carrot sticks on a plate. Encourage your child to make a little

45

cross in the top of her bowl of applesauce with her finger or spoon. Use this prayer for your Lenten cross meal: *ABCDEFG, Jesus gave new life to me.*

Sharing: During each week of Lent, add a couple coins to a plastic container with a childproof lid. The container creates a fun musical shaker for your child to shake while singing "Jesus Loves Me." Each week the sound and weight of the instrument changes a little with more coins. At the end of Lent, remove the saved-up coins and let your child place them in the offering.

 prek–k lower  upper

55. The central symbol of the Christian faith is the cross. This is an especially appropriate image for a Lenten journey with Jesus to his crucifixion. Families might choose to make or purchase a simple cross to hang in the area where they eat and have devotions. The cross can serve as a focal point for Lenten prayer that recalls the sacrifice of Christ that makes way for resurrection. Making the sign of the cross can be especially appropriate during Lent, when we remember our baptism and the mark of Christ through which we become Christians. By tracing the sign of the cross on our foreheads or bodies at the conclusion of each Lenten prayer, we remember our call to follow Jesus.

prek–k lower  upper

56. Along with Christmas and Easter, Pentecost is one of the three most important and celebratory days of the church year. Do not treat this Sunday as just another day! Pentecost demands we pull out all

the stops and go crazy with red (the "church" color for Pentecost): red crepe paper, red balloons, red tablecloth, red napkins, red candles, red juice as a beverage, a bowl full of strawberries. And naturally, of course, each family member should wear some item of red clothing. Do not underestimate the impact such preparations can make on children: this is a special—red letter—day! Here are more ideas:

- Read Acts 2:1-4 in your Bible.
- Sing "Happy Birthday" to the church.
- Make birthday cupcakes with crosses, flames (see Acts 2:1-4), or doves on them.
- Invite Sunday school friends, baptismal sponsors, or extended family to a party.
- Hang strips of red, orange, and yellow ribbon or crepe paper from the blades of ceiling fans (turned on low) for a visual reminder of the "wind" of the Spirit that came on Pentecost (Acts 2:1-4).

 lower upper

57. On All Saints Day, November 1, we remember and give thanks for those who have died in the faith of their baptism, as well as those who continue to live out their baptism in the midst of life now. Take a walk together in a nearby cemetery some time before or after All Saints Day. Wonder about the people buried there and stories the headstones might suggest. Share stories of members of your family and congregation who have died, especially stories about how they lived their lives of faith. Affirm the lives and service of those who now rest in God and the love they received from God throughout their lives.

 infant toddler

58. Before your baby can even understand the story of Pentecost or the significance of Lent, surround him with the symbolic color of these festivals or seasons. Dress him in red for Pentecost or Reformation Day, eat red foods, find all the red blocks or balls, buy red balloons, and use red crayons. During the "green" growing season in the time

48

after Pentecost, there are plenty of opportunities to find connections with green—trees, grass, flowers, clothes, even Oscar the Grouch or other familiar characters. Point out when they match the decorations at church!

infant toddler prek-k

59. Create a picture book with photos or cutouts from magazines or church newsletters and bulletins. Include symbols, colors, and illustrations from the current church season. In Advent, make the book with blue paper and include pictures of cradles, stables, donkeys, stars, even Christmas trees and presents to help tell your child the story of our Lord's birth. In Lent, use purple paper and add crosses, nails, crown of thorns, palm branches, a donkey (again!), an empty tomb, and Easter lilies. Take the book to church and connect your pictures with the surroundings in the worship and gathering spaces. Read the book at home to reinforce these and any other church seasons or other Bible stories.

Milestones and Special Occasions

all ages

60. Being a child of God calls for a celebration! Birthday parties celebrate being born; a baptism birthday celebrates being reborn as a child of God. Mark the anniversary of your child's baptism on the calendar. If you can't remember the date, call the office of the church where the baptism took place. Celebrate your child's baptismal birthday each year. Here are some ideas:

- Contact your child's godparents with a gentle suggestion that it would be very special if they called or sent a greeting.
- Invite your child's friends and baptismal sponsors.
- Light the baptism candle for a centerpiece at a meal.
- Place a bowl of water or a small fountain in the middle of the table. Use the water from it to place the sign of the cross on each other's foreheads.
- Share your memories and photos of the baptism day. Who was there? When the water splashed, did your child yelp, laugh, or sleep straight through it? Did she wear a special outfit? Did someone give a special gift?
- Ask your pastor for other resources to celebrate a baptismal anniversary.
- Encourage guests to bring canned goods to the party for donation to the food pantry.
- Say the Lord's Prayer together.
- If you have one, watch the video of the baptism.
- Sing songs: "Jesus Loves Me," "This Little Light of Mine," even Christmas carols no matter the season!
- Play "Pin Noah on the Ark."

Celebrating a baptism birthday gives your child a sense of how special it is to be not only a member of your family, but also a member of the family of God.

51

all ages

61. Write an annual letter to your child, dated on her baptismal anniversary. Write about the ways you have observed God at work in your child's life and growth, your family, and in the world. Express the hope and confidence you have in your child and in God as she continues to grow in the promises of baptism. Choose a milestone in the future—a confirmation, graduation, leaving home—to give her the letters as ongoing encouragement as she matures.

 toddler prek–k lower upper

62. Encourage love for God's word with the gift of a Bible on a baptism anniversary. The *Spark Story Bible* (age 2 to grade 2) and the *Spark Bible (NRSV)* (grades 3–6) are both attractive choices (both Augsburg Fortress, 2009). Ask godparents, Sunday school teachers, pastors, family, and friends to mark favorite stories and verses and to sign their names in the margins. Inscribe the front page with your child's baptismal date and a brief prayer or blessing from the giver. Include family members who live at a distance who can mark their selections through a parent. Continue marking the Bible each year to mark the baptism anniversary.

52

prek–k

63. Martin Luther said that through baptism we are all adopted by God. That's big news for adoptive parents. We already knew the miracle of God making us a family through adoption. Now we find out that God makes us an even bigger family with all Christians through our new birth with Christ. The next time we celebrate our child's adoption day, we can remind our adopted child that we are all adopted in God's eyes. Place a bowl of water in the middle of the table and make a cross on one another's foreheads, remembering that we are all beloved children of God. Thanks for the good news, Martin!

 infant  toddler

64. New teeth mean eating new things, and eating new things means checking out the practices of your church around holy communion. Talk to other parents and church leaders about when your child will begin receiving communion regularly. Many churches share the sacrament of communion with toddlers, and offer communion preparation classes to parents and their preschoolers. Get ready! It won't be long before your child reaches out with his hand and his questions.

53

prek–k

65. A Prayer for Beginning Kindergarten

Dear God, you know what an important day this is for *name* and for our whole family. Today *name* goes to big-kid school for the first time. When *name* was a tiny baby, you promised to love *him/her* and be with *him/her* forever. Then you helped *name* grow and grow, and now *he/she* is ready to go off to school. Thank you, God! This is wonderful! Go with *name* today, bless *his/her* learning, help *him/her* make new friends until, at the end of the day, we are all together again. Amen.

 upper

66. Dreading the first day of school or moving day? Are there other looming calendar days approaching—the end of being grounded, one-month mark of trouble-free school days, anniversary of losing a pet or grandparent? A few days before, decide on a bowl or box—decorated, plain, handmade, or purchased. Keep slips of paper and pencils near the container. Each family member can participate by recording messages of encouragement or thoughtful reflections. Alternatively, the messages can be just a single word, even a picture. On the big day, open up these notes and read them aloud together at the breakfast table or another time the family can gather. Allow your family to inspire further sharing of memories, reflections, or fears. When it feels right, finish this intimate family time by holding hands together and praying for peace, hope, strength, courage. Empower your child to lead this prayer with her own words. Or share a "popcorn" prayer to which each member of the group contributes a word, phrase, or petition. End with the Lord's Prayer or other family favorite.

 toddler prek–k lower  upper

67. Planning to move a child's bedroom or a whole house? Plan a house blessing or a room blessing to mark the ending of one thing and the beginning of a new thing. Family members take turns reading scripture and offering a prayer for each space as you journey from room to room. Symbols such as a candle or cross can be carried to recall that the life of the baptized is lived within these places. Water can be sprinkled in each space and finally on all the people gathered. The following examples may be used:

A child's bedroom
A reading from the Psalms: The LORD watches
over you; God will not fall asleep. (Psalm 121:5, 3)
Let us pray. O God, hold *name* in your unfailing love.
May *she/he* dream peacefully and grow in health and strength.
Bring *her/him* in safety to each new day. In Jesus' name we pray.
Amen.

(continued on next page)

A place where homework is done

A reading from Proverbs: To get wisdom is to love oneself; to keep understanding is to prosper. (Proverbs 19:8)

Let us pray. O God, you are the teacher who leads us to all truth. Grant that *those* who *learn* in this place may use knowledge to heal and help your world. Draw us together through our technology for every good purpose. In Jesus' name we pray.
Amen.

Additional prayers for the laundry room, living room, bathroom, and pet area may be adapted from *Evangelical Lutheran Worship Pastoral Care* (Augsburg Fortress, 2008) to use for the place where clothing is kept, toys and art materials used, and to include other areas your child enjoys.

Transitions

infant

68. Leaving your newborn with a caregiver can make a baby out of you! You drop off the baby then sit in your car and cry, telling yourself it will be okay. Prepare for these hard times with reinforcements—like "industrial-strength" prayers that God will care for your baby (and you!) in every place and time. Having a baby opens up a vulnerable place of love in us. We are so amazed at how much we can love our baby and so pained by how hard it is to be apart. God understands! God is with us in our hellos and good-byes. After all, God's story is a story of arrivals and departures. Jesus arrived on earth and had to say good-bye. But God sent us the Holy Spirit; we never have to be apart from God. So say good-bye, don't be afraid to cry, and find out what trust means.

 infant

69. Hugs are such a wonderfully tangible experience of love—physically surrounded, warmed, held, and protected. Teach your infant about hugs, both giving and getting. Use stuffed animals to demonstrate and label as you go: "Mama hugs kitty; baby hugs kitty!" "Mama hugs baby!" "Baby hugs mama!" Hugs from God and Jesus (through your arms) can help your little one relate to the "love" you keep singing and talking about. Hugs can now be given to family and friends, and can teach the first lessons in empathy and comforting ("Do you hear the crying baby? Maybe baby needs a hug!").

infant

70. Wrestling your little one into his car seat can be an exercise in patience, but if you have him participate by listening for the "clicks" as the safety harnesses buckle together, your child can begin to understand that these harnesses are just like a hug. Try this simple rhyme:

Here's a click to keep you safe!
Here's a click because God is great!
Here's a click for you-know-who!
God loves me and God loves you!

 toddler

71. Prayer and blessing can be helpful in easing difficult transitions. When your child moves to a "big kid bed," bless the new bed and offer a prayer for whoever will inherit her crib.

Stand over the new bed and say:
Dear God, Thank you for the blessings of home and rest. Bless your child *name* and *her/his big girl/big boy* bed. May *she/he* rest every night in your comfort and love. Amen.

Then stand over the crib and say:
Dear God, just as this crib has comforted *name*, may it now comfort Baby *name* as *she/he* sleeps. Please be with *her/him* as *she/he* grows and learns to live in your love. Amen.

59

toddler

72. Life happens all around your toddler, even if she is not directly involved. Your toddler will feel the difference in the air on that day when you find out your mom has cancer or you lose your job. And even if you barely know it, and your toddler only knows it uncon-

 sciously, your child is watching your face and your actions. Kids want to know, "Am I okay?" That's the same question we all have for God when life goes awry. Will we be okay? Be a model for your child. Go to God with that question, not just to a place of constant worry and fear. Go to your church friends and leaders with that question and seek their support. Witness to your child that your prayer will always be on the heels of your despair, and your community of faith sustains you.

 toddler

73. It can be hard for both toddlers and parents to say good-bye at the door of preschool or daycare. When it is time for you and your child to part, predictable and pleasurable rituals can help both of you. When leaving your child for the day, or before you go out for an evening, get down at your child's eye level. Mark a cross on his forehead and say, "Remember God loves you, and so do I." Your toddler can do the same for you. Or trace the sign of the cross in his open hand "because God loves you." Then put a "kiss to keep" in your child's hand "because I love you too." Fold his little fingers around it,

60

a handful of love that will last until you get back. Leaving one another in God's hands reminds us of who holds us 24/7. This good-bye ritual allows us to share our faith in a simple but powerful way.

 toddler prek-k lower upper

74. When custody arrangements mean that your child will be moving between parents, you want to keep the transition calm and predictable. Sharing a little prayer can become part of the leave-taking. If your child is concerned about anything, whether homework or a T-ball game, mention her need to God in prayer. Avoid turning concerns you may feel about your "ex" into a prayer in your child's hearing.

Dear God, I am so grateful for these good days we have had together, and for the good times *child's name* will have with *Daddy/Mommy*. Wherever *child's name* goes I know you are there already. Wherever I am, you are here with me too. I don't know how you do it, but I am so glad you will be with us both until we are together again. Amen.

 *lower*  *upper*

75. Give your child a simple blessing as she leaves for school in the morning. "God, sustain *name* in the gift of _____ by your Spirit today." Name one or more of the gifts of the Spirit from the blessing spoken over her in baptism: wisdom, understanding, counsel, might, knowledge, fear of the Lord, joy in your presence.

 *toddler* *prek–k*

76. The arrival of a new baby creates a perfect opportunity to talk about God's gracious love. Your child may be amazed by the helplessness of a newborn. Point out that the baby cannot hold his head up, or sit, or play, or chew. A baby can't do much that interests a child. That may be a disappointment for your child, but it's an opportunity for you. "Moms and dads love their babies even though they can't do anything. That's how God is too. We don't have to do anything to make God love us; God just does."

 lower

77. We all have sad days. When your child has such a day, bring out his baptismal candle. Light it. Draw your child close and look at the lovely light together. Begin by saying something like, "This candle can help you remember that God is with you no matter what happens.

62

You can talk to God about anything, anytime. Do you know that?" Your child might answer, or not. Hold him, or take his hand, and begin praying. "God, this has been a really tough day for *name*. The problem is _____ (*name the issue simply*)." Invite your child to tell God about it. Some children may speak; others may not. Whatever your child says to God in  prayer, do not interrupt or correct. You are teaching him it is safe to pour his heart out to God, who accepts your child as he is. Trust God to understand. When it seems your child is done, close with something like "Yes, Lord, this is a hard place. This candle reminds us how much you love *name*, especially right now. Wrap your arms around us; help *name* get through this. Thank you, Lord. Amen."

 upper

78. Create a family prayer journal to build intimacy and communication, especially during times of separation due to work shifts, busy schedules, travel, or military deployment. This can be a blank book, made with scrapbook supplies or purchased. It can also be created online using a social networking site restricted to your family members and supervised by a parent. Invite family members to write prayer requests and prayers in the journal. Once a week, during a family ritual time at meals or bedtime, pray for the requests and read any written prayers in the journal. The prayers in *Evangelical Lutheran Worship* on pages 72–87 are a good resource. Older children can be encouraged to select prayers to match the requests.

Church

 infant toddler prek–k

79. At baptism, we promise to bring our children to church. That can be a hard promise to keep. But we can actually lower our Sunday stress by making church a regular habit. When church becomes a given, we don't have to decide every week if we're going or not. We can spare our kids the association of church with should-we-or-shouldn't-we. Try singing this little rhyme to or with your child to the tune of "Twinkle, Twinkle, Little Star" as you are getting ready for church.

Stand up, sit down, sing and pray.
We are going to church today.

Jesus stories we will hear,
see our friends, and feel God near.

Stand up, sit down, sing and pray.
We are going to church today.

 infant

80. Make every worship service a sensory experience for your baby. Listen for words about God's love and hug your baby close. Notice when the sign of the cross is used by the pastors and trace it on your baby's forehead. During a baptism or when you see or hear a baptismal reference, "sprinkle" your baby all over with your fingers mimicking gentle water drops. During hymns, songs, and instrumental music, give your infant the opportunity to make a joyful noise by singing (both gently and boisterously!), clapping, dancing in your arms (swaying, bouncing), or "drumming" with a plastic spoon on

65

the pew, hymnal, or other surface. Rattles can add a festive sound to upbeat congregational songs while gentle rocking can underscore and emphasize the meditative and peaceful nature of other hymns. Be sure to sit somewhere where your child can see all the "action" of musicians, pastors, and other worship leaders.

 toddler

81. Teach your physically active toddler as many ritual gestures as you can! Make the sign of the cross. Mirror the pastor by extending one or both open hands in greeting ("The Lord be with you. And also with you."). Share the peace through handshakes and hugs. Pray with bowed heads, folded hands, or upturned open hands. Cup hands to receive the communion bread.

Help make worship a fun experience for your child by involving her in the most concrete and active parts of the service. This could include asking her to help you find page numbers for hymns, giving her coins or your family's weekly offering to put in the offering plate, or taking her with you to share the peace.

toddler

82. Take photos of some things in your church: pastor, cross, candle, font, altar, Bible, organ, piano, drums, hymnal, stained glass window, light fixture, artwork. Attach these photos to index cards or other heavy paper and bind them together with staples or metal rings (depending on how many cards you have). Or you could insert the photos into a 3" x 5" purse-sized photo album. You have now created a book that you and your child can read to learn the names of things in church. Bring your book along during worship and play I Spy by matching the things in the book to things in worship. To add interest, you may want to take the photos from a child's-eye view or take them from very close-up to show their details. To make this activity more challenging and keep it interesting, add photos of things with more advanced vocabulary such as stole, narthex or gathering space, sacristy, chalice (communion cup), and paten (communion plate).

 toddler prek–k

83. Many churches have a full baptismal font in the worship space during every service. These may look like miniature pools or fountains, and they are irresistible to little hands. The next time your toddler tries to reach up into the font, encourage him to do so. Teach him to draw the sign of the cross with water on your forehead and on his own. This gives your child an appropriate way to play in the water while reminding those around him of his baptism.

67

toddler prek–k lower  upper

84. When there is a baptism at your church, make sure your child has a front-row seat. Bring her to the front for a closer view, or plan to sit in front that day. After worship, share stories about how your child reacted to her baptism. Did she cry, squirm, sleep though it? Who was there to celebrate with her?

The next time someone of any age is baptized in your congregation, go home and help your child make a card to send to the newly baptized child of God. Invite her to use whatever colorful arts and crafts supplies you have on hand to make a card that says, "I'm baptized too! Welcome to God's family." Mail it promptly. You may find the address in your church directory, or contact your church office for assistance.

Older children could design an attractive baptism anniversary card to send to children in your congregation using drawings, photographs, or scrapbook techniques. Art can be scanned and printed on a color printer or reproduced by hand. Read the order for Holy Baptism in *Evangelical Lutheran Worship* (pp. 227–31) to find short words or phrases for the greeting, such as "Let your light so shine before others that they may see your good works and glorify your Father in heaven" or "Child of God, you have been sealed by the Holy Spirit and marked

with the cross of Christ forever." Ask the church office to provide names and baptism dates for sending the cards.

prek–k

85. Attending worship offers your kindergartner an opportunity to follow the words in a hymnal, see people of all ages, and begin to learn the liturgy by osmosis. But quiet worship also presents challenges for active kids. Here's one solution: Invest a few dollars in a spiral notebook and colored pencils. Lightly write *My Church Book* on the front of the notebook for your child to trace. Bring the notebook to worship. Encourage your child to "draw what you see." Reserve this notebook for church time only so it remains special. Give it to your child later as a confirmation gift.

Or create a busy bag that's filled with special toys and books that are only for use in worship. The bag might include a sticker book, board books, a stuffed animal, toy cars, crayons and a tablet of paper, or coloring books. Bring your child's picture Bible to church so that he can page through it during worship. When he is older, work with your child to make busy bags for other children to use.

 prek–k lower upper

86. Your children learn to worship by watching you. In worship, as you wait for others to have their turn at the Lord's table, you may find a "teachable moment." Ask, "Who belongs at the Lord's table?" Children's answers will vary, but the part you want to affirm is that all the baptized belong at the table; baptism is for belonging. Even if your congregation does not yet commune young children, bring your child forward for a blessing. Your child belongs.

69

 lower upper

87. Encourage children to follow along in worship by preparing them for what they may experience. Using *Evangelical Lutheran Worship*, locate the appointed prayer of the day and scripture readings (pp. 18–63). Look up one or more of the readings in a Bible. Read "Pattern for Worship" (pp. 92–93) and talk about your congregation's practices. If anyone in your family serves as a reader, usher, choir member, or assisting minister, make sure you point out the times when that happens. If your congregation worships from a worship book or worship folder, help your child to follow the service from it. Invite your child to draw pictures of changes in the worship space and what happens during worship throughout the church seasons.

 upper

88. Be on the lookout before, during, and after worship to see where you and your child can be of service to your congregation. Many congregations welcome parents and children serving together. Ushering together as a family unit can allow your child to serve others, welcome strangers, and participate actively in worship. Passing out bulletins, receiving the offering, preparing the communion table, and cleaning up after the service are all within your child's skill set and can only increase her appreciation for the rituals involved.

upper

89. Perhaps your child received a Bible in a formal ceremony at church; perhaps he has one from his baptismal sponsors. If he doesn't have one, get your child a Bible that he can write his name in and claim as his own. Have your child bring the Bible to church, find the scripture passages that are being read in worship, follow along, and mark pages or passages with bookmarks or highlighters, a bold way of showing how much of God's word they have heard. The *Spark Bible (NRSV)* comes with stickers and encouragement for marking verses and pages (Augsburg Fortress, 2009).

 upper

90. Children will grow in their understanding of being baptized into a community spread across time and culture by learning the stories of real people who lived through challenges to witness to their faith. Using the list of people commemorated annually by the church on pages 15–17 in *Evangelical Lutheran Worship*, research some of their stories on the Internet or at the library. Create a devotion book of their stories to give to members of the congregation on All Saints Day (November 1) or to use at family devotion times.

 upper

91. Older elementary children understand the meaning of promise making and promise keeping. If you promised a trip to the movie theater on Saturday, you can be sure that you'll be held to it! This is a good age to let your children know about the promises you made to God on their behalf. When your children were baptized, you promised:

> to live with *them* among God's faithful people,
> bring *them* to the word of God and the holy supper,
> teach *them* the Lord's Prayer, the Creed, and the Ten
>   Commandments,
> place in *their* hands the holy scriptures,
> and nurture *them* in faith and prayer.
> (*Evangelical Lutheran Worship*, p. 228)

As they get older, you can expect your children will have questions about how your family practices faith. Why do we go to worship? Why do I go to Sunday school? Why do you want me to start confirmation classes? Because you promised God, and meant it. Because you take your responsibilities seriously. Because, more than anything, you want your children to grow into strong, faithful adults who trust God and care for others and the world God made.

72

World

toddler   prek–k

92. Although your child is very young, it is not too early to lay the foundations in her for sharing, caring for others, and caring for the world. Toddlers, preschoolers, and kindergartners love to help, and helping others will start to teach these values. Watch your newspaper, church newsletter, bulletin, or congregational Web site for service opportunities that you and your child can do together. These could include filling school kits with school supplies for needy children, delivering meals to homebound people, visiting care facilities, donating to the food pantry, helping at church cleanup days, or doing a short charity walk together.

infant

93. Want to witness love in action? Talk to your pastor about older church members confined at home or in a care facility. Ask who might benefit from a visit by you and your baby. It's amazing to watch people come to life when a baby arrives. When you share your baby, you are sharing love. And it's not just the older person and the baby who will benefit. Your visit will further connect you to the generations in your church community, teach you about sharing, and exercise your baptismal call to be a partner with God in this world.

toddler   prek–k

94. Make grocery shopping trips more fun and meaningful for your child by inviting him to pick out items to donate to the food pantry while you shop. Your child may like to pick out some of his favorite foods to donate. Check with your local food pantry for a list of current needs if you are uncertain about what items would be most useful. Finding the items on the list will be like a scavenger hunt for your child. Bring your child along when you drop off the food.

toddler   prek–k   lower

95. Keep some blank note cards handy, and when your child is looking for paper to color or paint on, offer her the blank cards. From time to time, ask your child to name someone who might appreciate a greeting. Encourage your child to think about those who are sick, in need of cheering up, or deserving of thanks. Ask questions such as, "Who is someone we could thank for helping us this week?" or "Who did we pray for in church today?" Then use one of the predecorated note cards to send a piece of your child's original artwork to that person.

75

lower

96. Seek out an "adopted grandparent" relationship with an elderly member of your congregation or a resident in a nearby retirement community. Commit to at least a year of monthly visits. Help your child ask his/her "grandparent" about their life and stories, and to share events in his own life. Structure a simple activity: bring a game to play together, a book your child can read aloud, or the lesson from Sunday school for your child to share. Pray together at the end of the visit, perhaps asking both the "grandparent" and your child, "What would you like to pray about each other today?" In relationships like these, your child experiences the larger family of God to which we belong in baptism.

 *lower* *upper*

97. Vacations provide great opportunities to exercise care for others and the world God made because we see new places with fresh eyes. Consider spending part of a day volunteering in your favorite vacation spot. If your trip will take you near a wildlife refuge, learn about their work beforehand and ask if there is volunteer work your family can do. Pick up litter around campsites or on a beach. Locate a homeless shelter in a town or city and ask if there is a chore you could do together as a family. Returning home, you will see the familiar with new eyes and see new opportunities to care for others and the environment where you live.

 upper

98. As older children encounter a world in need of justice and peace, help them gain confidence in questioning. Resist the urge to answer every question. Cultivate questions that invite deeper conversation and exploration of faith active in service: "What do you think?" "What would you do?" or "I wonder what would happen if . . . " or "What is God doing in this?"

 upper

99. Read together to engage older children in conversations about living out their baptismal faith. Look for more complex characters in fiction, history, or biography who are both gifted and faulted, who experience a change of heart and forgiveness, or who exercise a sense of mission or purpose to work for good for humanity and creation. The reluctant reader may enjoy listening to audio books together at bedtime or in the car. Christian themes may not be explicit, but your conversation will open ways to talk about God's work in the world.

upper

100. In baptism, we pass from death into life with Jesus. Every day we are called to die to our old life of sin and rise to the new life Jesus calls us to live. As children grow, they become increasingly aware of troubling news in the world and in their own communities. In baptism, we know that troubles come, but God's love and desire for new life is made visible in our lives of grace. Empower your child to respond to the concerns that trouble her by looking for the new life growing up from the old. News about families losing homes can translate into sorting the outgrown toys in the family and taking them to a family homeless shelter. If your family eats out frequently, help your child calculate how much could be saved by making a simple meal together at home and contributing the savings to an organization that addresses hunger or responds to disasters. Invite an older child to participate in the family's decisions about sharing resources with those in need and designating charitable giving.